Janaki, Art and Scooter are waking up from a long sleep. They have never met before.

"Uh?!"

"Where am I? Who are you?"

"Who are you?"

They do not understand what is happening to them. Where are they?

All of a sudden the screen begins to flicker. A long, thin face peers down at them.

Listen to me now! I am Zardoz! You will do as I tell you!

They start to talk, and find out that they all play football. Is this why they are here?